WHAT A FIND!

A Problem-Based Unit

**The College of William and Mary
School of Education
Center for Gifted Education
Williamsburg, Virginia 23185**

WHAT A FIND!

A Problem-Based Unit

The College of William and Mary
School of Education
Center for Gifted Education
Williamsburg, Virginia 23185

Center for Gifted Education Staff:
Project Director: Dr. Joyce VanTassel-Baska
Project Managers: Dr. Shelagh A. Gallagher
Dr. Victoria B. Damiani
Project Consultants: Dr. Beverly T. Sher
Linda Neal Boyce
Dana T. Johnson
Dr. Jill D. Burruss
Amy B.K. Muraca
Donna L. Poland

Teacher Developer:
Francis T. Cawley

funded by Jacob K. Javits,
United States Department of Education

KENDALL/HUNT PUBLISHING COMPANY
4050 Westmark Drive   Dubuque, Iowa 52002

Copyright © Center for Gifted Education

ISBN 0-7872-2608-4

Kendall/Hunt Publishing Company has the exclusive rights to reproduce this work,
to prepare derivative works from this work, to publicly distribute this work,
to publicly perform this work and to publicly display this work.

Printed in the United States of America
10 9 8 7 6 5 4 3

CONTENTS

Part I

INTRODUCTORY FRAMEWORK

INTRODUCTION

What a Find! is a problem-based science unit designed for high ability learners which has been successfully used with all learners in a wide variety of situations, from pull-out programs for gifted learners to traditional heterogeneously grouped classrooms. It allows elementary students to explore archaeology in a novel way, namely through the process of grappling with an ill-structured, "real-world" problem.

Because the unit is problem-based, the way in which a teacher implements the unit will necessarily differ from the way in which most traditional science units are used. Preparing for and implementing problem-based learning takes time, flexibility, and a willingness to experiment with a new way of teaching.

The total time required for completion of *What a Find!* should be minimally 30 hours, with more time required for additional activities.

RATIONALE AND PURPOSE

This unit has been designed to introduce elementary students to archaeology. The problem-based learning format was chosen in order to allow students to acquire significant science content knowledge in the course of solving an interdisciplinary, real-world problem. This format requires students to analyze the problem situation, to determine what information they need in order to come up with solutions, and then to find that information in a variety of ways. The problem-based method also allows students to model the scientific process, from the problem-finding and information-gathering steps through to the evaluation of data and the recasting or solution of the problem. In addition to problem-based learning, the unit also depends upon the overarching scientific concept of systems, which provides students with a framework for understanding the civilizations whose remains are preserved in archaeological dig sites.

GOALS AND OUTCOMES

➡ To understand the concept of systems

Students will be able to analyze several systems during the course of the unit. These include the archaeological "problem system," historic systems, and culture systems.

SYSTEMS OUTCOMES

A. For each system, students will be able to use appropriate systems language to identify boundaries, important elements, input, and output.

B. Students will be able to analyze the interactions of various system components with each other and with input into the system.

C. Students will analyze several systems during the course of the unit. These include the natural system of which a dig site is part and the culture whose artifacts are preserved in an archaeological dig site.

D. Students will be able to transfer their knowledge about systems in general to a newly encountered system. In the final assessment activity, students will be given a new system to analyze in the same way that they have analyzed the systems in the unit.

➡ To engage in scientific research

In order to solve these scientific problems, students will be able to design, perform, and report on the results of a number of experiments.

SCIENTIFIC PROCESS OUTCOMES

A. Students will be able to explore a new scientific area, namely archaeology.

B. Students will model the scientific process through problem-based learning.

C. During their scientific work, students will:

—Demonstrate good data-handling skills

—Analyze data as appropriate

—Evaluate their results in light of the original problem

—Use their enhanced understanding of the area under study to make predictions about similar problems whose answers are not yet known to the student

—Communicate their enhanced understanding of archaeology to others

➡ To understand the principles of archaeology

SPECIFIC CONTENT OUTCOMES

A. Students will become familiar with the general goals and methods of the discipline of archaeology.

B. Students will learn the uses of archaeology tools including data-recording equipment such as the notebook and camera, and excavation equipment, such as trowels and brushes.

C. Students will investigate various archaeological dating methods.

D. Students will visit a real archaeological dig and observe archaeologists at work.

ASSESSMENT

This unit contains many assessment opportunities that can be used to monitor student progress and assess student learning. Opportunities for formative assessment include:

- Student problem logs, a written compilation of the student's thoughts about the problem. Each lesson contains suggested questions for students to answer in their problem logs. The problem log should also be used by the student to record data and new information that they have obtained during the course of the unit.

- Experimental design worksheets, which can be used to assess a student's understanding of experimental design and the scientific process, as well as to record information about what was done and what was found during student-directed experimentation.

- Other forms which are used to help the student explain solutions to particular parts of the problem.

- Teacher observation of student participation in large-group and small-group activities.

- Final unit assessments, which allow the teacher to determine whether individual students have met the science process, science content, and systems objectives listed in the Goals and Objectives section at the beginning of the unit.

SAFETY PRECAUTIONS TO BE TAKEN IN THE LAB

As this unit involves laboratory work, some general safety procedures should be observed at all times. Some districts will have prescribed laboratory safety rules; for those that do not, some basic rules to follow for this unit are:

1. Students must behave appropriately in the lab. No running or horseplay should be allowed; materials should be used for only the intended purposes.

2. No eating, drinking, or smoking in lab; no tasting of laboratory materials. No pipetting by mouth.

3. If students are using heat sources, such as alcohol burners, long hair must be tied back and loose clothing should be covered by a lab coat.

4. Fire extinguishers should be available; students should know where they are and how to use them.

MATERIALS LIST

Materials needed for each individual lesson are listed in the "Materials and Handouts" section of the lesson.

LESSON FLOW CHART

Problem-based learning is not easy to plan, because it is driven by student questioning and interest. We have included estimated durations for each lesson in this unit, but be prepared to be flexible and to move with the students. We have also included a diagram (Figure 1) which shows the relationship between and among the individual lessons in the unit. In general, lessons shown higher in the diagram are prerequisites for those shown lower in the diagram.

FIGURE 1
LESSON FLOW CHART

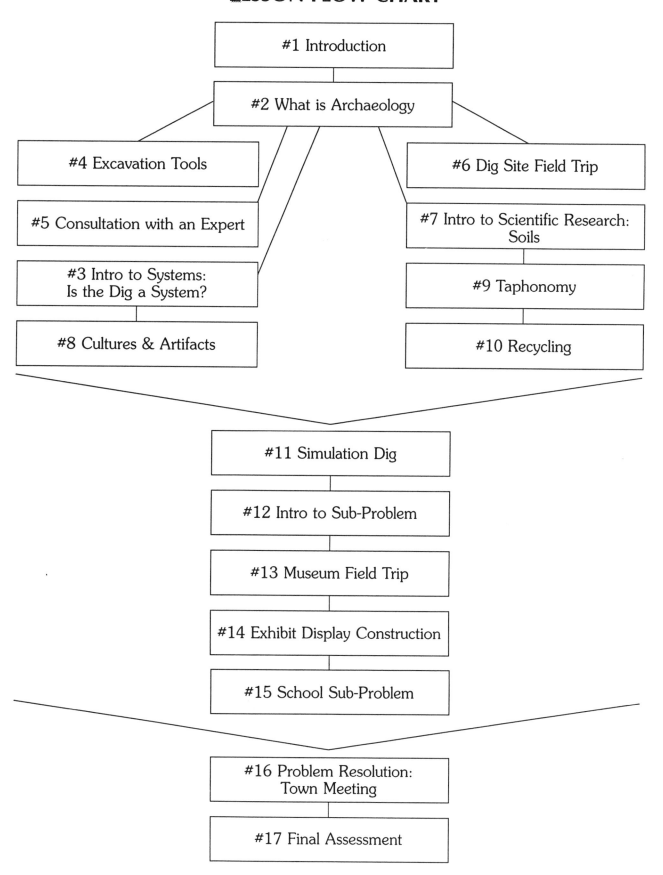

#1 Introduction

#2 What is Archaeology

#4 Excavation Tools

#5 Consultation with an Expert

#3 Intro to Systems: Is the Dig a System?

#8 Cultures & Artifacts

#6 Dig Site Field Trip

#7 Intro to Scientific Research: Soils

#9 Taphonomy

#10 Recycling

#11 Simulation Dig

#12 Intro to Sub-Problem

#13 Museum Field Trip

#14 Exhibit Display Construction

#15 School Sub-Problem

#16 Problem Resolution: Town Meeting

#17 Final Assessment

CODE OF CONDUCT

Archaeological sites are a non-renewable resource which can yield priceless information about the everyday lives of people and cultures. These sites, and the information and artifacts that they contain, hold clues to larger cultural puzzles. Trained professionals need to examine these clues *in situ*—or in place—in order to decipher their hidden meaning.

Sites that have been dug, or partially dug, by even the best intentioned "history buff" lose most, if not all, of their research potential. Once a site has been dug, it is destroyed, and if not dug right the first time, is lost forever. The information the site held is gone as well.

Since the cultural and historical information gained from archaeological sites can be accessed in no other way, and since it can tell us about people for whom we have no first-person documentation, this information is valuable to everyone. Poor peoples, prehistoric peoples, and slaves have all left their marks in the dirt, if not on paper. Archaeologists hold these sites and this information in a public trust, and pass along new information in many ways. Public lectures, conference papers, books, journals, and magazines are some examples. Public education programs and excavation classes are also presented to the public.

Please, don't dig on your own, and don't encourage children to dig. Stress the importance of resource management and protection. There is plenty to study and do in archaeology without digging up a yard. It gives students the wrong idea about archaeology. Remember, it's not as simple as "finding the stuff"—it's not a treasure hunt of randomly scattered artifacts. Professional archaeologists carefully gather clues using a systematic approach and scientific method. If scattered holes are dug and things are simply buried in the ground at random depths, in random isolated pockets, not only are the existing layers being contaminated, but the central concepts of archaeology are missed. The layers of an archaeological site, and the holes that cut them, are studied to determine events and relative dates. The artifacts located in specific layers and features leave specific information about people and events. They help to date to a specific time and explain an event.

Design projects that don't oversimplify archaeology. Real artifacts are related to each other and tell a meaningful story about our past.

Amy Muraca
Staff Archaeologist for
Colonial Williamsburg Foundation

GLOSSARY OF TERMS

Archaeology: The scientific study of material remains of past human life and activities.

Artifact: A characteristic product of human activity; usually a hand-made object (as a tool or ornament) representing a particular culture or stage of technological development. Examples include flint arrowheads, pottery, personal computers.

Boundary (Systems): Something that indicates or fixes a limit on the extent of the system.

Culture: The customary beliefs, social forms, and material traits of a racial, religious, or social group.

Dig Site: An archaeological excavation site.

Element (Systems): A distinct part of the system; a component of a complex entity (system).

Excavate: To expose to view by digging away a covering.

Input (Systems): Something that is put in the system; an addition to the components of the system.

Interactions: The nature of reciprocal connections made between/among elements and inputs of a system.

Output (Systems): Something that is produced by the system; a product of the system interactions.

Ruins: The remains of something destroyed.

Scientific Process (or Research): The scientific research process can be described by the following steps:

1. Learn a great deal about your field.
2. Think of a good (interesting, important, and tractable) problem.
3. Decide which experiments/observations/calculations would contribute to a solution of the problem.
4. Perform the experiments/observations/calculations.
5. Decide whether the results really do contribute to a better understanding of the problem. If they do not, return to either step 2 (if you're very discouraged) or step 3. If they do, go to step 6.
6. Communicate your results to as many people as possible.

Stratum: A layer or a sheetlike mass of sedimentary rock of earth of one kind, lying between beds or on beds of another kind.

System: A group of interacting, interrelated, or interdependent elements forming a complex whole.

Taphonomy: The study of the way things are preserved and the effects of burial.

LETTER TO PARENTS

Dear Parent or Guardian:

Your child is about to begin a science unit that uses an instructional strategy called problem-based learning. In this unit students will take a very active role in identifying and resolving a "real-world" problem constructed to promote science learning. Your child will not be working out of a textbook during this unit but will be gathering information from a variety of other sources both in and out of school.

The goals for the unit are:

- *To understand the concept of "systems."*

  Students will be able to analyze several systems during the course of the unit. These include the "problem system" centered around an archaeological area and the historical and cultural systems involved.

- *To understand the principles of archaeology.*

  Students will understand the specific methods and principles employed by archaeologists to investigate a dig site.

- *To engage in scientific research.*

  In order to solve scientific problems, students need to be able to engage in research study. During their work, students will:

  —Demonstrate good data-handling skills

  —Analyze data as appropriate

  —Evaluate their results in the light of the original problem

  —Use their enhanced understanding of the area under study to make predictions about similar problems whose answers are not yet known to the student

  —Communicate their enhanced understanding of archaeology to others

Since we know from educational research that parental involvement is a strong factor in promoting positive attitudes toward science, we encourage you to extend your child's school learning through activities in the home.

Ways that you may wish to help your child during the learning of this unit include:

- Discuss systems, including family systems, educational systems, etc.

- Discuss the problem they have been given.

- Engage your child in scientific-experimentation exercises based on everyday events such as: In a grocery store, how would you test whether it's better to go in a long line with people having few items or a short line with people having full carts?

- Take your child to area science and historical museums and the library to explore how scientists solve problems.

- Use the problem-based learning model to question students about a question they have about the real world, e.g., How does hail form? Answer: What do you know about hail? What do you need to know to answer the question? How do you find out?

Thank you in advance for your interest in your child's curriculum. Please do not hesitate to contact me for further information as the unit progresses.

Sincerely,

Part II

LESSON PLANS

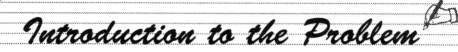

Introduction to the Problem

LESSON LENGTH: 2 sessions

INSTRUCTIONAL PURPOSE

- To introduce students to a problem to be explored throughout the unit.

MATERIALS AND HANDOUTS

A drawing or picture of an unearthed foundation/or

Numerous shards of uncertified ceramics or "glass"/or

Numerous bones or bone pieces (animal)/or any combination of the above

Handout 1.1: Problem Statement

Handout 1.2: "Need to Know" board

Handout 1.3: Problem Log Questions

Handout 1.4: Problem Log Questions

Session 1

THINGS TO DO

1. Hand out the Problem Statement (Handout 1.1) and have students read it in class.

2. Organize the Problem Statement into three categories on the "Need to Know" board: What Do We Know, What Do We Need To Know, and How Can We Find Out. Prioritize the Need to Know list from most to least critical.

3. As students generate questions for the "Need to Know" board, ask them to tell why the information is important or what idea they are pursuing by asking for the information.

4. Debate reasons for prioritizing choices. Ask students to identify resources that will help them answer or further investigate the elements of the Need to Know list. Divide the learning issues among students so that each student (or a different group of students) will bring different information to the class on the following session.

THINGS TO ASK

- What's going on?
- What are we supposed to do?
- What seems to be the main problem?
- What seems to be the key pieces of information?
- Why is this a problem?
- Are there other problems?
- Why did they stop work on the school?
- Where can we find the answers to these questions?
- Do you have any ideas right now about what to do?

Session 2

THINGS TO DO

1. Provide the "artifacts" for students to look at. Have them identify new key pieces of information from the study of the artifact. Allow time for some in-class research if necessary, or assign a "task force" to go to the library to gather more information.

2. Have students report on the information they found overnight. Ask them to look over the "Need to Know" board and identify: 1) what questions they have answered; and 2) what new questions arise out of their new information. Next, ask students what they are going to need to know in order to solve the problem. Prioritize the list based on negotiations with students.

THINGS TO ASK

- What questions are answered by the new information?
- What questions do we still have to answer?
- What new questions do you have?
- What are the things we may have to learn about to solve the problem?
- Is the problem different today than it was yesterday?
- How are we going to solve this problem?
- What sort of strategies should we use?
- What will the different stages of our job be?
- How will you know when the problem is solved?

ASSESSMENT

Paraphrase the problem situation in the Problem Log.

HANDOUT 1.1

PROBLEM STATEMENT

You are an archaeologist working as an intern at a local research museum.

Your supervisor has just received a call from a local construction site. While doing construction to build a new school, construction workers found numerous artifacts. They halted construction and need to know what to do next. Your supervisor has assigned you the task of figuring out what is going on.

HANDOUT 1.2

"NEED TO KNOW" BOARD

What do we know?	What do we need to know?	How can we find out?

PROBLEM LOG QUESTIONS

As intern archaeologist, your job is to figure out what's going on at the construction site. Based on what you know right now, what do you think is going on? What's the problem?

Write a list of questions that are important to answer in order to solve the problem.

1. _____

    _____

2. _____

    _____

3. _____

    _____

4. _____

    _____

5. _____

    _____

6. _____

    _____

2

What Is Archaeology?

LESSON LENGTH: 2-3 sessions

INSTRUCTIONAL PURPOSE

- To help students understand the process of excavating a dig.

MATERIALS AND HANDOUTS

Video or film, e.g., *Doorway to the Past* or *Archaeologists at Work*

Resource materials on archaeology, e.g., *Dig This! How Archaeologists Unearth Our Past*

(See references for specific information and additional suggestions, text-books, etc.)

Handout 2.1: Problem Log Questions

Session 1

THINGS TO DO

1. Ask students what they will "Need to Know" in order to conduct a dig at the site where the artifact was found. Generate a list of questions, probing for students' prior knowledge of digs, or their intuitions about how a dig would be conducted (What We Know or What We Think We Know).

2. Review the "Need to Know" board and discuss questions about how an archaeologist operates in the field and how a dig site is set up. Students should generate questions about conducting an excavation.

3. Assign different questions to individuals or to small groups of students. Allow research time for students to find the answers to the questions.

THINGS TO ASK

- What were some processes used by the archaeologists?

- Why were those processes so important?

- What special tools were used by the archaeologists?

- Would any of this information about an excavation have meaning to our problem?

- What might happen to the school building site if a full scale excavation were started?

Session 2

THINGS TO DO

1. Divide class into groups and assign each group an archaeological process to research such as mapping a site, cataloging a site, taking notes at a site, preserving and packing specimens.

2. Have a group or the whole class watch a video on archaeology (e.g., *Doorway to the Past*) and have students note processes used by archaeologists in the field.

3. List the processes used by archaeologists. Divide students into groups and have each group research a different process. Groups should prepare a presentation on their topic, for the class as a whole, to be given later in Session 3.

THINGS TO ASK

- Why is your group's particular process important?

- What special things does an archaeologist have to do in your process?

- How might your process be important to our understanding of what we have to do with our dig?

Session 3

THINGS TO DO

1. Bring the class back together for a large group discussion. Have students report on the process they were assigned, addressing the questions they were researching and the answers they found. Review the "Need to Know" board to see which questions were answered by the information they gathered. Generate new questions raised by the new information. Review the problem definition to see if it needs re-defining in light of the new information.

2. Reports made by students should lead to discussion about archaeological techniques and what scientists do in order to get information from a site.

3. Start a concept map with the first student report. This can be done on large butcher paper so that you can refer to it in the days ahead. As each report is finished, have the class decide where on the concept map the new information belongs. By the time the reports are complete, students should have a concept web that demonstrates how the various archaeological processes fit together. Discuss with students whether or not the whole map represents a system.

4. Discuss the next steps towards excavating the dig. Ask students to decide whether it is better to just go and do the dig or whether they want to learn more or even practice some techniques first. Generate a list of additional learning issues and/or things to practice.

THINGS TO ASK

- How might your assigned process help reveal a part of history?

- How does all this information change the way you think about our problem?

- What's the best way to proceed now? Should we just go out and do the dig or are there some more things you want to learn or practice doing?

- Why might practicing be a good idea?

- What are some of the skills you have to practice before going out and doing a real dig?

ASSESSMENT

1. Group report presentations and archaeology concept map.

2. Problem Log Questions.

HANDOUT 2.1

PROBLEM LOG QUESTIONS

A lot of new information has emerged since the problem was first presented to you. Go back and look at your original problem statement. Do you think that the problem has changed? Why? Why not? What do you think the exact problem is now?

Introduction of Systems Concept: Is the Dig a System?

LESSON LENGTH: 1 session

INSTRUCTIONAL PURPOSE

- To introduce the concept of systems.

MATERIALS AND HANDOUTS

Chart paper

Handout 3.1: System Parts Chart

THINGS TO DO

1. Guide students through a brainstorming session that addresses the question "What is a system?" Ask students in small groups to come up with several examples of a system. Then have them generalize about their understanding of systems. (Students should be able to describe a system as made up of elements and movement.)

A system is a collection of things and processes that interact with each other and together constitute a meaningful whole. Examples from the realm of science include atoms, chemical reaction systems, individual cells, organs, organ systems, organisms, ecosystems, solar systems, and galaxies; nonscience examples include sewer systems, political systems, the banking system, transportation systems, and so on. All systems share certain properties. These include:

a. Systems have identifiable elements.

b. Systems have definable boundaries.

c. Most systems receive input in the form of material or information from outside their boundaries and generate output to the world outside their boundaries.

d. The interactions of a system's elements with each other and their response to input from outside the system combine to determine the overall nature and behavior of the system.

2. Create a list of student-generated examples of systems (e.g., the digestive system, the solar system, the interstate highway system). Discuss similarities among the systems.

3. Have students generate examples of things that are *not* systems. What new insights does this exercise provide about understanding a system?

4. In small groups, ask students to state or find definitions for terms associated with systems: boundary, elements, input, output and interactions. Have students apply this information to one or two of the systems they listed as examples.

5. Reconvene as a total group to discuss student findings.

6. Ask students to list the components of an archaeological dig. Ask if the dig could be considered a system. List student responses on chart paper. Encourage use of proper systems terminology.

THINGS TO ASK

- What are some systems you can think of? How do you know that it's a system?

- What are some general things we can say about systems, based on our discussion so far?

- What do all of the systems you can think of have in common?

- List all of the parts of our archaeological dig you can think of. Do you think these are parts of a system?

- What part of the dig represents the boundary? Elements? Input?

- How can understanding systems help us keep track of what's going on in the dig?

ASSESSMENT

System Parts Chart (Handout 3.1).

HANDOUT 3.1

SYSTEM PARTS CHART

1. What are the boundaries of the system? Why did you choose them? Were there other possibilities?

2. List some important elements of the system.

3. Describe input into the system. Where does it come from?

4. Describe output from the system. What part(s) of the system produce it?

5. Describe some important interactions:
   a. among system elements

   b. between system elements and input into the system.

6. What would happen to the system if the interactions in 5a could not take place? In 5b?

Excavation Tools

LESSON LENGTH: 1 session

INSTRUCTIONAL PURPOSE

- To understand appropriate uses for a variety of archaeological tools.

MATERIALS AND HANDOUTS

Archaeological tools (or photos of tools), such as:

*notebook with graph paper	plumb bob
*camera	shovel
video camera	bucket
tape measure	brush
trowel	dust pan
screen box	line level
candy canes	string

(*items are essential)

Handout 4.1: Problem Log Questions

THINGS TO DO

1. Break class into small groups. Give each group a tool or tool photo.

2. Ask them to infer or guess the use of their tool. If they can think of multiple appropriate uses for this tool, ask them to list them.

3. Have students research the actual use of their tool, using the archaeology resources materials in the classroom.

4. Have the groups report their results to the class. List the tools and uses on the board. Have students copy it into their problem logs.

THINGS TO ASK

- Why are fancy tools important? Why not just dig artifacts up with a backhoe or shovel?

- Are there multiple ways to use tools?

- Which tool would be best to excavate a broken plate? an arrowhead? a cannonball?

- How can we use this information?

- Why do we need a notebook/camera?

EXTENSIONS

Bring in some old tools and antiques. Ask the class to come up with uses for these tools. Then debrief.

PROBLEM LOG QUESTIONS

1. Describe the tool your group researched and its uses.

2. If you were an archaeologist, which tool would you like the best? Why?

Consultation with an Expert in Archaeology

LESSON LENGTH: 3 sessions

INSTRUCTIONAL PURPOSE

- To provide interaction with a professional working in archaeology.

MATERIALS AND HANDOUTS

Chart and Markers

Audio-Visual equipment for guest speaker

Handout 5.1: Visitor Planning Sheet

Session 1
Before the Speaker Comes

THINGS TO DO

1. Brainstorm with students, deciding what questions need to be asked of the speaker. Use the "Need to Know" board to choose questions.

2. Class discussion can help sort questions into most and least important questions.

3. Students should also be guided to think about the best way to phrase the questions. Are they specific enough? Are they too specific?

4. Group questions can be recorded on a master question chart.

5. Students can then add any of their own questions to individual Visitor Planning Sheets (Handout 5.1).

THINGS TO ASK

- What information do we want to know?

- What information will the guest speaker be most qualified to give?

- What do we want to know by the time the guest speaker leaves?

- What facts do we want to get from this person?

- What opinions would be interesting to have?

- Which of these questions are most important?

- How can we get an idea of this person's perspective on this kind of situation?

- Do you think this person will have a bias? What would it be? How can we find out?

Session 2
The Guest Speaker's Presentation

THINGS TO DO

1. Guest Speaker: The guest provides his/her information regarding archaeology.

2. Students take notes and ask their questions.

3. Students should also be prepared to share with the guest speaker background on the problem and their decisions to date.

Session 3
Debriefing

THINGS TO DO

1. In a follow-up to the guest speaker, teacher and students should review the "Need to Know" board, removing questions which have been answered and adding new issues, if necessary.

2. Teachers and students should discuss the potential bias in the information provided by the guest speaker and the possible effects of that bias on the validity of the information.

THINGS TO ASK

- What were the things we learned from the guest speaker?

- How does the new information affect our thinking about the problem?

- Do we need to reorganize our approach to the problem?

- Did this person reveal a particular bias? If so, what?

- Where can we go to get another perspective? A balanced report of information?

ASSESSMENT

1. Students should report in their problem logs information provided by the guest lecturer and reflect on the potential of bias.

2. Students write a thank you letter to the guest speaker, detailing which information was particularly helpful.

HANDOUT 5.1

VISITOR PLANNING SHEET

Student Name _____

Name of Visitor _____

Who is this visitor?

_____

_____

_____

Why is this visitor coming to see us?

_____

_____

Why is this visitor important to us?

_____

_____

_____

What would you like to tell our visitor about our problem?

_____

_____

What questions do you want to ask the visitor?

_____

_____

_____

lesson

6

Dig Site Field Trip

LESSON LENGTH: 3 sessions

INSTRUCTIONAL PURPOSE

- To provide an opportunity for students to observe an operational archaeological dig.

MATERIALS AND HANDOUTS

Chart paper for listing questions

Handout 6.1: Field Trip Questions

Handout 6.2: Problem Log Questions
Handout 6.3: Problem Log Questions
Handout 6.4: Problem Log Questions

Session 1

THINGS TO DO

1. Review the "Need to Know" board for questions that still need to be answered. Brainstorm a list of questions students would like to have answered on the field trip.

2. Group questions according to perspective (e.g., from an archaeologist's perspective; a landowner's perspective; an artifact finder's perspective, etc.).

3. Prepare class for trip by discussing what students expect to see; give them Handouts 6.1 and 6.2 so they'll know what to look for and think about.

4. Select a class photographer(s); review procedures for taking good photos. Select a class "scientific" artist to draw/sketch the site.

THINGS TO ASK

- What questions would you like answered during our field trip?

- If you were brought in as a consulting archaeologist, what information would you want to know about this excavation?

- What if you were a local townsperson, what would you want to know?

- If you had been planning on building a house on the site, what would you want to know?

- How can we clarify the boundaries, elements, interactions, inputs, and outputs of the dig site as a system?

Session 2

THINGS TO DO

1. Visit an archaeological dig site and talk with resident archaeologist(s). Students should ask the archaeologist their questions. One student should keep track of the main question list to make sure that all of the important questions are asked.

2. Under the supervision of the resident archaeologist, allow students to look at the site. Artists and photographers should record the information which the group thinks is most important.

Session 3

THINGS TO DO

Back in the classroom, review what students learned during their time at the dig. Ask students to use all of the information they have learned since the problem was presented to generate a "plan of attack" to get the dig excavated. Tell students to use their problem log worksheets to help recall ideas and organize their thoughts.

ASSESSMENT

Problem log entry about the field trip site.

1. An archaeologist might have many questions that need to be answered about a dig. (Example: What kind of artifacts might be found there? What kind of tools do I need to excavate the site? How big of an area needs to be mapped out? How many people do I need to work on this dig?) List some more questions an archaeologist might have.

2. The owner of the land where the site is located may have many questions. (Example: How long will it take to excavate the site? How much land will they use? Who will own the artifacts that are found on the land?) List some more questions a landowner may have concerning an archaeology dig located on his/her land.

3. A person who finds artifacts may also have many questions concerning the dig. (Example: What tools do I need to use? How do I tag the artifact? How do I determine whether or not something is an artifact?) List some more questions artifact finders may have.

Draw a map of the archaeology dig site you observed. Think of the site as a system. Label all parts of the system. Include boundaries, elements, inputs, outputs, and interactions you saw at the dig.

What kinds of information were they uncovering at the dig? What kind of time period were they finding out about? Think of one artifact you saw on the field trip and discuss how that artifact fits in the time period.

HANDOUT 6.4

PROBLEM LOG QUESTIONS

List what you have learned about archaeology thus far that will help you formulate a plan for doing an excavation.

Introduction to Scientific Research: Soils

LESSON LENGTH: 2 sessions (a third optional lesson)

INSTRUCTIONAL PURPOSE

- To develop a definition for "soil."
- To allow students to investigate the different types of soils, characteristics of soils, and soil profiles.
- To consider the impact of soil loss on humans.
- To consider the role of undisturbed soils in the dating of artifacts.

MATERIALS AND HANDOUTS

Samples—sand, loamy soil, clay, humus, gravel, generic potting soil, cactus soil, African violet soil, local garden soil (whatever soil is locally available), perlite, vermiculite, peat moss

Tablespoons or other measuring devices such as ¼ cup measures or small disposable paper cups, paper towels, hand lens, small clear glass jars with lids, water

Handout 7.1: Observation of Soils

Handout 7.2: Soil Characteristic Sheet
Handout 7.3: Problem Log Questions
Handout 7.4: Problem Log Questions

Session 1

THINGS TO DO

Before class: Collect materials, make certain that the samples are well separated and that spoons or other measuring devices are next to each sample. Label each sample with a number and keep a list of the samples and their associated sample numbers.

During Class:

1. Break the class into small teams. Ask each team to obtain and label a small sample of each different type of soil you have provided. (Or ask each team to take only one type of sample and then compare results across teams rather than within teams.)

2. Ask them to verbally and visually describe each sample as viewed with the naked eye. Then ask them to use a hand lens and describe (verbally and visually) what each looks like using that instrument. Ask the teams to decide which samples are "soil" and which aren't, providing supporting evidence for the decisions. Ask each team then to develop a definition for "soil" and finally to compare their definition to others and to formal ones in science texts and dictionaries.

3. Have the students record their descriptions (written and drawn) on the Observation of Soils (Handout 7.1) and hypothesize the composition of each sample. Clean up sites and wash hands.

4. Put the names of each sample type on the board or overhead and determine how close the team descriptions were to the actual samples.

5. Have the class discuss the formation of soil from rocks and how it might vary according to geographic location. A diagram showing the weathering of rocks and the addition of humus and organisms would be useful to develop at this time.

6. Have the class brainstorm a list of all the reasons soil is important to humans.

7. Optional: Determine if there are living organisms in your local soil samples by placing a small sample of local garden soil on a piece of gauze or cheesecloth and place it in the mouth of a glass funnel resting in a clean glass jar. Leave the jar with the funnel in it under a light over night. The light will move the organisms into the funnel and then into the glass jar. Have the students look at the organisms using a hand lens or magnifying glass and then ask that students draw sample organisms for their records. Some students might want to check the materials with a microscope or attempt to label the organisms.

Suggestion: Call your county extension agent and see if someone might come to class (or talk to the class on the phone or on Internet) to discuss local soil types, agriculture, and erosion practices in the local area.

THINGS TO ASK

- What do you think "soil" really is? What does soil look like to the naked eye? What does it look like under a hand lens?

- How are these descriptions different or similar?

- Do any of the samples appear to be composed of particles of only one type of material? Which ones? How can you tell this?

- Do any of the samples appear to be composed of anything other than small particles of rock? If yes, what might this material be and why? What might be the source of this material? (This material is typically organic matter and must be present for the samples to technically be considered "soil.")

- What is "soil" composed of? Is it the same everywhere? Why might it be different in different parts of the county? (The students might want to develop experiments to determine how and why soils are different in different locations?)

- How long does it take to develop soil? How thick is the "soil" in our local area? Soil depths do vary. Why might its depth vary according to location?

- What *type* of soil is common around here? Why do you believe that is true? How might we check to see if your guess is true?

- Why is soil important to people? What would happen if we had no soil or if we ruined the soil we had?

- What does this exploration of soils have to do with archaeology?

Session 2

THINGS TO DO

Before Class: Collect and label different soil samples

During Class:

1. Assign a soil type (or multiple types) to each team. Ask them to collect at least a quarter of a cup of the material(s) and bring it back to the team's table. There the students are to complete a Soil Characteristic Sheet (Handout 7.2) on their type or types of soils, using both unaided observation (naked eye) and land lens.

2. Have the students place approximately two tablespoons of their sample in a small glass jar. They are to add approximately half a cup of water, close up the jar and shake the jar for a minute. After letting the jar sit for a few minutes (the soil materials will settle out according to general type with loam or humus floating on top and sand settling onto the bottom, finer clay particles will probably be in suspension in the water until they have enough time to later settle out on top of the sand) the students are to describe the different layers that form in the jar over the next few days of observation (example: immediately, an hour later, next day, two days later). Compare and discuss the teams' findings following completion of this activity. Complete Handout 7.2.

3. Discuss how knowing the layer of soil or dirt might aid the archaeologist in dating an object.

THINGS TO ASK

- How can you scientifically compare soil types? What general characteristics are useful in the comparison and what ones are not useful?

- What is a soil profile? What is a soil horizon? How are they similar and different?

- What are the different soil horizons and how do they differ?

- How are soils and types of plants that grow in them connected? Are certain soil types best for certain types of agriculture? What examples can you present to support your case?

- What are some human activities that destroy soils and prevent the development of new ones? Are there any local examples of such soil loss? What is causing or contributing to that loss? How do you know that? Might there be a different cause? Can you brainstorm some other possible causes for the soil loss? How might you prevent additional soil loss?

- How might an archaeologist use soil horizon information to date an artifact? What might s/he ask or investigate if artifacts are found when a farmer is digging up a field?

Optional Session 3
(Field-trip with discussion)

THINGS TO DO

Visit a recent road cut or place where the different soil horizons and layers are observable. Ask the students to describe (verbally and visually) the horizons and/or layers and hypothesize why they look the way they do. Or if that is not possible, bring in soil cores from various areas for student to observe and describe. Or visit a newly turned field and discuss how plowing or construction disrupts soil layers and horizons and how an archaeologist might deal with that disruption

ASSESSMENTS

1. Problem log entry about soils.
2. Problem log entry about soil types and profiles.
3. Accuracy of Handout 7.1.
4. Accuracy of Handout 7.2.

EXTENSION ACTIVITIES

1. Permeability or percolation studies on soil samples.
2. Farming practices and soil conservation.
3. Erosion or soil loss.
4. The great Dust Bowl or current desertification.
5. Siltation in mouths of rivers and loss of topsoils.
6. Destruction of rain forest soils.
7. Overgrazing practices.
8. Soil-less gardening.
9. Composting

NOTE TO TEACHER

If students have studied weathering (mechanical and chemical) of rock materials, effects of climate on weathering, decomposition, take the time prior to this lesson to review weathering. If students have not studied weathering, then now is an opportune time to study these subjects.

Description of sample #1:

Drawing of sample #1:

Description of sample #2:

Drawing of sample #2:

Hypothesis on composition of the soil sample:

Definition of "Soil":

Sample #1:

    color

    texture

    smell

    particles making up sample

    organisms

Type of Soil?

Reason for choice of type?

Drawing of a soil horizon: Label each layer.

Handout 7.3
Problem Log Questions

1. What is soil and what role does it play in the archaeologists' task?

2. What type of soil is common to our locality and how might one recognize it? How does this information help clarify the problem?

HANDOUT 7.4

PROBLEM LOG QUESTIONS

1. Suppose the archaeologists have been called to a site and find that all the layers of artifact-bearing soil have been disturbed by heavy equipment. How might they determine what the typical soil profile is in that area?

2. What suggestions or recommendations might you make to a construction company so that this matching task might be easier to do?

Cultures and Artifacts

LESSON LENGTH: 3–5 sessions

INSTRUCTIONAL PURPOSE

- To enable students to understand cultures as systems.

MATERIALS AND HANDOUTS

Index cards

Yarn

Interaction cards (developed by the teacher)

Resource materials

Handout 8.1: Cultures as Systems

Handout 8.2: Problem Log Questions

Handout 8.3: Problem Log Questions

Session 1

THINGS TO DO

1. Pick a culture (anything from ancient Assyria to modern USA). Use a culture that you might already be studying (e.g., American Indians, Egyptians, etc.)

2. Define its:

   boundaries (space it occupies)

   elements (particularly focus on subsystems: should include at a minimum transportation system, food production system, political system, economic system, religious beliefs).

   List existing *input* (e.g., products entering through trade—imports of products, ideas, art, culture)

   List existing *output* (e.g., products leaving through trade—exports of products, ideas, art, culture)

THINGS TO ASK

- How is a culture like a dig? List the things they have in common.

- How is a cultural system unlike a dig system?

- How might a dig reveal the system of a culture?

- How do artifacts help us understand the system of the culture?

Sessions 2–3

THINGS TO DO

1. Have students research the cultural system elements that they found in the dig in detail; assign students to groups to learn as much as possible about each element of the particular system they are studying.

2. Make a bulletin board with index cards representing each researched element. Students can summarize information about the element they studied and share their information with the class as each index card is posted onto the board.

3. Have each group link its element to the other elements that it interacts directly with using pieces of string. A complex web should result, showing students that no element in the system can function by itself.

THINGS TO ASK

- Look at the artifacts you found. What do the different artifacts do?

- How does each artifact add to our understanding of culture?

- If these are a part of a system, which part would they be (input, output, elements, boundary)?

- How do elements affect each other?

- Do these elements always stay the same? Why? Why not?

- What makes them change?

Sessions 4–5

THINGS TO DO

1. As a class, discuss an interaction that affects one element of the system. Either new input into the system (e.g., new invention, new kind of food crop, new disease) or a change in an existing subsystem (e.g., crop failure, military coup) could be used.

2. Have a member of the student group responsible for the affected subsystem describe the effect of the interaction in its group's subsystem.

3. For each of the elements to which the affected subsystem is linked, have a member of the appropriate student group discuss the effects of the change in the affected subsystem on that group's element.

4. As a group, summarize the overall effect of the perturbation on the system as a whole.

5. Assemble small groups of students composed of a representative from each of the different culture elements. Have each group choose three or four interaction cards. Interaction cards include *new input* or *alterations* affecting a particular element of the culture. Examples for our culture might include: war, flu epidemic, new form of mass transit, sudden death of President, drought, war, contact from a foreign country. Interaction cards need to be created by the teacher as appropriate for the culture under study. *Different* interaction cards should be given to each small group.

6. Have each group work through the consequences of the first interaction and describe the changed culture that results.

7. Have students choose a second interaction card and work through the results on the changed culture that had just been described. Then do a third and perhaps a fourth level interaction.

8. At the end of the session, have the class reconvene and have the different small groups report on the interactions and the final shape of their culture. (Posters, charts and other visual aids could be developed by groups to illustrate the changed elements of the culture.) The final cultures that resulted in each group should be different, giving students a feeling for the processes that result in the evolutionary change of a culture.

THINGS TO ASK

- Why was each group's final culture different?
- What might a dig system reveal about a culture system?
- What might a dig system not reveal about a culture system?

ASSESSMENT

Group reports of culture system changes.

HANDOUT 8.1

CULTURES AS SYSTEMS

Boundaries: Geographical boundaries of a culture, set up to include all of its elements.

Elements: 2 sets

    Physical

    buildings

    roads

    people

    animals

    Cultural

    language

    religion

    political

    economic

Input: Physical or cultural items from outside (new religion, foreign money, invading armies, new agricultural practices, etc.)

Output: Physical or cultural items shipped to outside.

Interaction: Trade, politics, etc.

PROBLEM LOG QUESTIONS

1. Is it important that cultures change? Why? Would we need archaeologists if cultures didn't change? Why? Why not?

2. Could a culture *not* change over time? Why or why not?

HANDOUT 8.3

PROBLEM LOG QUESTIONS

How do findings from the dig help us understand a cultural system? Can a single artifact be a part of the dig system and a part of a cultural system? How? Choose an artifact and use it as an example in your answer.

Taphonomy

LESSON LENGTH: 1 session introduction; 1 session conclusion with several weeks of time for the experiment to take place.

INSTRUCTIONAL PURPOSE

- To teach experimental design through taphonomy.
- To help students understand the elements of experimental design including hypothesis, independent variable, dependent variable, constants, data and conclusions.

MATERIALS AND HANDOUTS

Article on taphonomist Anna Behrensmeyer*

Flower pots

Various soils (e.g., dry sand, potting soil enriched with cow manure—some with water added and without water)

Sample materials (e.g., plastic, iron nails, galvanized nails, wood, orange peel, carrot peelings, metal scouring pad, etc.)

Handout 9.1: Memorandum

Handout 9.2: Taphonomy Experiment Chart

Handout 9.3: Questions on Article

Handout 9.4: Problem Log Questions

Handout 9.5: Student Brainstorming Worksheet

Handout 9.6: Student Experiment Worksheet

Handout 9.7: Student Protocol Worksheet

Handout 9.8: Laboratory Report Form

*Behrensmeyer, A. K. (1992). Speaking out. *Science*, 255, 1388.

THINGS TO DO

1. Discuss techniques archaeologists use and have students read article in *Science* about taphonomist Anna Behrensmeyer. As a group, discuss role of a taphonomist.

2. Ask how taphonomy might be important to the dig problem. Taphonomy is the study of the way things are preserved, such as the effects of burial.

3. Discuss how class could design an experiment to test effects of the environment on materials.

4. Present a chart of the experimental design that lists each part: title, hypothesis, independent variable, dependent variable, constants, control, data, and conclusion. Talk about taphonomy and ask how the class might test effects of the environment on materials and then develop an experiment with students, giving examples of each part as the experiment is developed. Use an experimental design chart to detail each decision made about the experiment.

5. Create an experimental design to test the effect of soil on various materials. (See Handouts 9.5, 9.6, and 9.7.) Distribute laboratory package and as a group design an experiment to test the effects of soil on deterioration of artifacts. Variables could be soil type; amount of water added over time; materials buried; or temperature range.

6. A good record of materials before burial is a photograph. Have the class photographer take pictures of all the materials to be buried prior to conducting the experiment.

7. Have students fill in their Experiment Worksheets (Handouts 9.5–9.7) as the discussion proceeds.

8. Depending on the hypothesis selected by the class, students should predict which types of conditions would favor preservation of all materials, hinder preservation, or which materials would be preserved the longest.

9. Students will need to gather data on soil effects in this experiment in several weeks (the longer that objects can be buried in soil, the more likelihood of observable change).

10. Conclusions about the experiment can be drawn from the data at the end of the several week experiment. As students discuss their conclusions, they relate the data to the problem.

THINGS TO ASK

Questions will relate to the specific experiment the teacher chooses to conduct. For example:

- What do you think will happen if we could bury objects for a year? Ten years? One hundred years? One thousand years?

- Why?

- What might change?

- Do all objects change the same way?

- Look at the artifacts we've gathered. Did these artifacts look like this when they were new? How do you think they looked when they were first made?

- What made these artifacts deteriorate?

- Do you think that being underground speeded or slowed the deterioration (or made no difference)?

- What other changes could being in the ground make?

- Why would it be important to understand the effects of the soil on the artifacts?

- Why would it be important to know about the preservation of materials?

- How is taphonomy an important part of archaeology?

- List ways the results of the experiment impact the school site dig.

Important: NEVER misinterpret the results of an experiment in order to "fit" a convenient conclusion. If an experiment gives unexpected data, discuss why this might have happened and how students should proceed with this unexpected result.

ASSESSMENT

1. Experiment design.
2. Lab reports.

EXTENSION ACTIVITY

Students can investigate further information about the study of taphonomy and perform independent taphonomy experiments.

MEMORANDUM

Before you begin . . . the Museum Director wants to know that you are following the proper laboratory practices. Write a memo to the Director describing the safety practices you will follow during your experiment:

M E M O R A N D U M

To: The Museum Director

From:

Re: Safety Practices

Date:

HANDOUT 9.2

TAPHONOMY EXPERIMENT CHART

Date	Soil/Water Type	Size of Object	Observations

HANDOUT 9.3

QUESTIONS ON ARTICLE

1. Are there words or ideas in this article that you don't understand? Where could you go or what could you do to help you understand? List the words or phrases that you don't understand. Discuss how you will find the information you need.

2. What is taphonomy?

3. Why do you think Anna Behrensmeyer's professor did not think women should do field work?

PROBLEM LOG QUESTIONS

Congratulations! You finished your experiment!! All scientists feel good after finishing an experiment, but they also always think about how they could do the experiment better next time.

1. How do you think you could do your experiment better next time?

2. What parts would you keep the same?

STUDENT BRAINSTORMING WORKSHEET

1. What do we need to find out? (What is the scientific problem?)

2. What materials do we have available?

3. How can we use these materials to help us find out?

4. What do we think will happen? (What is our hypothesis?)

5. What will we need to observe or measure in order to find out the answer to our scientific question?

Adapted from: Cothron, J. G., Giese, R. N., & Rezba, R. J. (1989). *Students and research.* Dubuque, IA: Kendall/Hunt Publishing Co.

HANDOUT 9.6

STUDENT EXPERIMENT WORKSHEET

Title of Experiment:

Hypothesis (Educated guess about what will happen):

Independent Variable (The variable that *you change*):

Dependent Variable (The variable that responds to changes in the independent variable):

Observations/Measurements to Make:

Constants (All the things or factors that remain the same):

Control (The standard for comparing experimental effects):

STUDENT PROTOCOL WORKSHEET

1. List the materials you will need.

2. Write a step-by-step description of what you will do (like a recipe!). List every action you will take during the experiment.

3. What data will you be collecting?

4. Design a data table to collect and analyze your information.

LABORATORY REPORT FORM

1. What did you do or test? (Include your experiment title)

2. How did you do it? For materials and methods you can go to your Student Protocol Worksheet (Handout 11.10) and use the information from the first two questions.

3. What did you find out? (Include a data summary and the explanation of its meaning)

4. What did you learn from your experiment?

5. What further questions do you now have?

6. Does the information you learned help with the problem?

Note to Teacher: Following are the answers to brainstorming experiment and protocol student worksheets.

TEACHER ANSWERS TO BRAINSTORMING WORKSHEET

1. What do we need to find out? (the scientific question)

   We need to find out what happens to different materials when they are buried in wet soil.

2. What materials are available?

   Soil

   Sample Materials including: old socks, tin cans, bubble gum and other artifacts of the modern age

   Plant pots and saucers

   Water

3. How can we use the materials to help us find out?

   Bury the samples in the dirt in the plant pots for awhile; keep the dirt wet and see what happens.

4. What do we think will happen? (hypothesis)

   The appearance of some of the objects will change; other objects will be relatively unaffected.

5. What will we need to measure/observe?

   We will need to compare the appearance of buried samples of the materials with the appearance of unburied samples of the materials.

TEACHER EXPERIMENT ANSWER SHEET

Title of Experiment: What is the impact of burying an object in soil for a *period of time?*

Hypothesis: If we bury objects in soil for several weeks, they will change appearance.

Independent Variable: Soil types.

Dependent Variable: Size and color of objects.

Constants: Pot size, soil type, amount of soil, amount of water.

Data: Measurement, color, and descriptive observation of objects to be buried.

Conclusion: Depends on what happens during the experiment.

TEACHER PROTOCOL ANSWER SHEET

Materials and equipment:

> *Soil*
>
> *Sample Materials including: old socks, tin cans, bubble gum and other artifacts of the modern age*
>
> *Plant pots and saucers*
>
> *Water*

Procedure:

1. Put one sample of each material into its own plant pot. Put the duplicates in a safe place.

2. Cover the materials in the pots with soil.

3. Water daily for 3 weeks with 20ml of water per pot.

4. After 3 weeks, dig up each sample. Compare the appearance of the buried sample with the unburied duplicate sample; record observations in the data table.

Data Tables: In this case, data tables would take the following form:

Object	Appearance of buried sample	Appearance of unburied sample

Recycling

LESSON LENGTH: 2 sessions

INSTRUCTIONAL PURPOSE

- To understand the concept of solid waste and its connection to archaeology.
- To explore different ways of disposal of waste materials and their impact on life systems.
- To explore different ways to recycle materials.

MATERIALS AND HANDOUTS

Clean empty 2 liter soda bottles (cut off top) one per team

Soil

Samples (visible food scraps like egg shells or bread, metal pop top tab, plastic top, piece of cloth, styrofoam cup, piece of paper bag or newsprint, etc.) (each team should use 3 or 4 samples at most)

Thermometers

Plastic wrap

Rubber bands

Session 1

THINGS TO DO

Before Class: Collect materials, prepare the cut bottles.

During Class:

1. Have students build a model landfill and investigate what happens to various materials after burial in the dirt. Students should fill in a prediction sheet prior to developing this landfill. Have the students:

    - Fill the bottle half way with soil.

- Using graph paper, trace the outlines of all the samples they will be using. Label each material and make notes on any special characteristic of the material.

- Place the materials one at a time in the bottle. Cover each material with soil.

- Add enough water to the soil so it is damp but not wet.

- Place a thermometer in the bottle so it can be read and seal the bottle with plastic wrap and a rubber band. Move the bottle to a dark location and let it sit for the next few weeks.

- Record temperature of the "landfill" every day for two or three weeks. Record the temperature at the same time of day for each reading.

- After the desired amount of time has passed, remove the plastic wrap, remove each of the materials and trace the new outlines of each on another sheet of graph paper. Compare the sizes of each of the items with their original size and descriptions. Also note any other differences in the soil or the air of your landfill. Compare your predictions to the findings. Can you come up with possible reasons for the differences?

- Wash up carefully and dispose of all items as instructed by the teacher.

2. Have the students design a new experiment using different materials and stressing prediction of anticipated results. Compare wet soils to dry soils, warm temperatures to cool temperatures.

THINGS TO ASK

- What things decomposed? Which ones decomposed the most . . . based on what evidence? What problems are created by those materials that show no signs of decomposition?

- What did the decomposing? What factors influence this process?

- What are some of the by-products of decomposition? How do we deal with those problems?

- What happens if the weather is cold and/or extra rainy?

Session 2

THINGS TO DO

1. Have the students determine and record all solid waste (trash) material they create during a typical day. They should record that on a daily journal sheet of their own design.

2. Using their journal entries, students should then analyze which materials might be recycled and which ones could not be (with reasons given for these decisions).

3. Ask that students brainstorm a list or lists of common items of "trash" and common items that are recycled locally.

4. Debate the issue of "Paper or Plastic."

THINGS TO ASK

- What is solid waste? How does your family dispose of its solid waste? How is municipal solid waste disposed of locally? What other ways are used nationally to dispose of this waste?

- What does NIMBY mean? (Not In My Backyard) Why is it a common concern related to waste disposal?

- What is the problem with the growing use of plastics? How is it a different problem from the one associated with the use of aluminum cans or glass bottles? What is degradable plastic and how long does it take to degrade?

- What is the difference between biodegradable and non-biodegradable? Why is this question important for archeologists?

- What are our options for the future? How can you help with these solid waste problems?

- What solid waste do you believe is typical at your favorite local fast food restaurant? How might you research this question? How might you reduce the amount of trash waste from this restaurant? Does this place already engage in recycling activities . . . if so what are they and how are they working for this company?

- What does recycling do to the dating procedures of archeologists of the future? Could the same problems exist looking at older cultures today?

ASSESSMENT

1. Problem Log (Handout 10.1) questions on landfills.
2. Problem Log (Handout 10.2) questions on recycling.
3. Preparation for and participation in the debate on "Paper or Plastic."

EXTENSION ACTIVITIES

1. Hazardous waste disposal
2. Ocean dumping of waste materials
3. Incinerators
4. Profitability of recycling
5. Highway use of recycled materials
6. Old tire waste
7. Composting
8. Debate the merits of building housing developments on landfills
9. Investigate environmental policies related to waste materials at the Federal, state, and local levels

HANDOUT 10.1

PROBLEM LOG QUESTIONS ON LANDFILLS

1. Frequently archaeologists find the dumps of specific people (potters, tavern keepers, etc.) or cultures (middens). These can be rich areas to explore because they can tell a lot about a people and their customs and practices. What would your garbage tell about you and your family?

2. What problems do landfills pose to growing populations and what are some of the ways those problems are being addressed?

PROBLEM LOG QUESTIONS ON RECYCLING

1. Recycling is not a new concept. What evidence do you have that it has occurred in earlier times?

2. Should we use materials that are non-biodegradable? Support your answer.

3. Should we have strict container laws? . . . even if it means people are put out of work?

Simulation Dig

LESSON LENGTH: 3 sessions

INSTRUCTIONAL PURPOSE

- To simulate an archaeological dig.

MATERIALS AND HANDOUTS

Mini Dig Site Materials:
Large plastic shoe boxes
Sand
Soil
Peat moss
Vermiculite

Student Lab Tray Materials:
Lab shirts for student protection
Spoons
Brushes
Magnifying glasses
Handiwipes
Plastic tarps for floor
Probe
Site booklets
Buckets
Goggles
Surgical gloves
Sifter (can be made by cutting
a hole in the top of a box and
covering opening with wire mesh)

Sample Artifact Materials:
Prehistoric
Arrowheads
Pot shards
Deer bones

Colonial Period
Brass buttons
Copper coins
Barley seed
Headless nails
Glass
Animal bones
Seeds
Ceramics

20th Century
Plastic strapping
Rubber hose
Paper clips
Styrofoam

Handout 11.1: Site Book
Handout 11.2: Archaeology
Handout 11.3: Safety Procedures

Handout 11.4: Simulation Dig
Handout 11.5: Artifact Chart
Handout 11.6: Problem Log Questions

Before Class: Teacher should prepare simulation dig sites by filling large plastic-lined shoe boxes (or other similar containers) with four strata of sand, soil, peat moss, and vermiculite on top. Each stratum should be seeded with different artifacts from a specific time period. Prehistoric (up to 1600); colonial period (1600–1800) and 20th century (1900–present).

THINGS TO DO

1. Discuss what can be revealed by an archaeological dig. Discuss how a culture is revealed. What might this have to do with the problem we are trying to solve?

2. Review procedures for conducting a dig with students. Ask students to outline, step by step, their plans for excavating the digs. Students should include the specific roles each member of the team will play as a part of their plans. Be sure to talk about **safety procedures** including reasons to wear smocks, gloves and goggles.

3. Students can be assigned to archaeological teams. Each team can be given a box to excavate. Students should excavate stratum by stratum (remember lesson on soils and stratification), collect, record and classify all artifacts.

4. After excavating the artifacts from each stratum, students should sift the soil for any undiscovered artifacts.

5. After artifacts are unearthed, they need to be classified according to some criteria. Discuss with students ideas about how to classify the artifacts. Historical period (age of the artifact or stratum in which the artifact was found) should be one of the criteria considered.

6. As elements of the system are unearthed, possible interactions should be predicted.

7. Data and observations should be recorded in Archaeology Site Books.

8. After children complete their dig, reconvene class to discuss findings and piece together evidence from the cultures.

THINGS TO ASK

- How are you going to go about getting things out of the dig?

- What are the steps that real archaeologists follow?

- How are we going to make sense of all the artifacts that we found today?

- What are the different ways we could group these artifacts?

- What gives clues about what happened in the past?

- Do the artifacts from each time period fit together in some way?

- Could they act as a system? What would the boundaries, elements, inputs, outputs, interactions be?

- How does the archaeological system help decode history?

- What new information do we have to help us with the problem?

- Does the problem look different now than it did before?

ASSESSMENT

1. Teacher observation of excavation procedure.

2. Archaeology Site Book.

EXTENSIONS

1. The U.S. Government Booklet 24-5-00528, *Above Ground Archaeology*, provides another interesting way to simulate the process of excavating an archaeological dig.

2. Arrange a visit to an archaeological site that will allow students to actually participate in the "dig." Prior to the visit, discuss with the archaeologist the history or background of the site, and the skills students will be able to practice. For the students, discuss how an archaeologist operates in the field. Discuss archaeological techniques, reviewing information from the video students previously watched, the reports students had done on archaeology process techniques, and the various experiences they have had. Include a review of good safety practices for a field archaeologist to observe.

THINGS TO ASK

- What artifacts did you find?

- What did you discover about an archaeological dig? Was the outside excavation similar to our simulation dig? How? How was it different?

- Were there any problems setting up the boundary of your dig system? Why?

- Did you discover any evidence of interactions among the dig elements?

- Was there any input to or output from the dig system?

- Was soil stratification evident? How did your understanding of soil stratification aid in your understanding the artifacts' relationship to one another?

115

ARCHAEOLOGIST:

_____

NAME OF DIG:

_____

Steps Used by an Archaeologist:

1. Look for clues on the surface.

2. Mark off the surface of the site.

3. Dig the entire surface of a square as a unit.

4. Sift the soil.

5. Note change in the soil.

6. Tag each artifact, noting the original position in the ground by using the name of the square and the number of the level in the square.

7. Carefully brush and clean the artifacts.

8. Map the profiles of the artifacts.

HANDOUT 11.3

SAFETY PROCEDURES

Before you begin:

List the safety procedures we discussed in class and state why each safety rule is important.

1. _____

   _____

   _____

2. _____

   _____

   _____

3. _____

   _____

   _____

4. _____

   _____

   _____

Handout 11.4

Simulation Dig

1. Excavate one stratum at a time:
   a. Remove soil stratum to bucket.
   b. Clean artifact.
   c. Number artifact.
   d. Record data—strata (1, 2, 3)
   e. Sift soil for small artifacts.

2. What are the artifacts you found? What are they made of? How might they have been used?

_____

_____

_____

_____

What A Find!

Handout 11.5

Artifact Chart

Artifact	Quadrant Where Found	Possible Age Of Artifact	Possible Use Of Artifact	Questions or Notes

HANDOUT 11.6

PROBLEM LOG QUESTIONS

What is the most important discovery you made about archaeology on your mini-dig? How did you make this discovery? What was the hardest part of this dig? Why? What did you learn that will be important to remember when you get to the real dig?

Introduction to Exhibit Sub-Problem

LESSON LENGTH: 1 session

INSTRUCTIONAL PURPOSE

- To extend students' skills in independent study.

MATERIALS AND HANDOUTS

Sub-Problem Statement (taped message)
Resource materials on museums; museum displays
Cassette Player

Handout 12.1: "Need to Know" board
Handout 12.2: Problem Log Questions

THINGS TO DO

1. Bring a cassette tape player to class with a telephone message recorded onto it (see attached message). Have students listen and take notes to see what the message means to them as an intern archaeologist.

2. Use the "Need to Know" board to list the information presented in the tape and the additional information which students want to find out. Allow some students to do some quick "search and scan" research of materials in the room to answer basic information questions.

3. Discuss the relative merits of doing the museum display. Ask students what additional kinds of materials they will need in order to develop a museum display along the lines suggested by the funding agency.

4. Have students list the tasks which will have to be completed in order to get the display prepared and the resource people that should be contacted to make sure

that they do the job in the right way. Although students will come up with many ideas, they should see a need for some information in at least two general areas: 1) current culture and 2) setting up a museum display.

THINGS TO ASK

- What is the purpose of the telephone message?

- What were the details of the message?

- Do you think you heard everything the first time?

- What good would come to the museum if we completed the project?

- Do you think it's a good idea? Why? Why not?

- Do we have everything we need to do a museum display on past and present cultures? What else will we need to do?

- How can we find out how to do a museum display? Who could help us figure out what to do?

- If there is such a thing as an artifact of a past culture, could there be an artifact of a culture today? What kinds of things would be artifacts?

- How should we organize this new list of things to do and to find out?

ASSESSMENT

Problem Logs.

SUB-PROBLEM STATEMENT

(Best if presented as a recorded telephone message)

Hi, Joyce, this is Felicia Crossett calling from the Springwater Foundation. I'm calling because I think I have a pretty exciting offer for you. It seems we have a little extra money in the budget this year, and since I heard you just found some interesting new artifacts in the new dig you've been working on, I thought I'd offer you first dibs. I'm ready to subsidize a museum display based on your new finds. As you know, the Springwater Foundation has as a major goal helping people understand past history. I would like for the museum display to focus on two things in particular. First, it should focus on something like "Linking the Past to the Present." Second, to add to the educational nature of the display, I would like for it to describe the process of conducting an archaeological dig. Let me know if you're interested in this opportunity—I really think that it will give you a chance for some good publicity and perhaps some money from other sources as well. Give me a call soon! Bye.

HANDOUT 12.1

"NEED TO KNOW" BOARD

What do we know?	What do we need to know?	How can we find out?

What are your ideas for doing a museum display that would be titled "Linking the Past to the Present"? How could we use artifacts to compare the past and the present?

lesson

Museum Field Trip

LESSON LENGTH: 3 sessions

INSTRUCTIONAL PURPOSE

- To provide an opportunity for students to observe an operational museum and the ways it links the past to the present.

MATERIALS AND HANDOUTS

Chart paper for listing questions

Handout 13.1: Problem Log Questions
Handout 13.2: Problem Log Questions

Session 1

THINGS TO DO

1. Use the "Need to Know" board to generate questions about what information is needed about putting together a museum display to reveal a culture and how it was discovered.

2. Have students decide which questions could be answered through a visit to a local museum.

3. Students can generate specific things they can look for in a museum for help in doing their own displays and generate specific questions to ask a museum curator and docent about their work.

THINGS TO ASK

- What questions would you like answered during our field trip?

137

- How will you remember the information you learn on this field trip?

- What will you be looking for at the museum?

Session 2

THINGS TO DO

1. Visit a historical museum and if possible, arrange to talk with both the curator and a docent.

2. Have students ask their questions about how museums create displays to present information about the past, and how they demonstrate the processes that were used to make the discoveries that are presented.

3. Students should be encouraged to take notes and/or draw pictures of display ideas.

Session 3

THINGS TO DO

Back in the classroom, review what students learned during their time at the museum.

THINGS TO ASK

- How did the museum demonstrate the linkage of the past and the present?

- What were some display techniques that worked especially well?

- What were some display techniques that seemed problematic?

- How were the curator and docent jobs similar? Different?

- How will the information found during our trip be helpful in your own museum display preparations?

ASSESSMENT

Problem Log entries about the field trip to the museum.

EXTENSIONS

1. Another good resource person for students to contact would be a foundation representative. Interested students could find out why foundations give money to people and why organizations participate in philanthropic activities.

2. Students could explore historical museum sites on the Internet. How is the information presented differently from an actual museum? What are the advantages and disadvantages of each type of exhibit?

HANDOUT 13.1
PROBLEM LOG QUESTIONS

What did you learn about museum displays? What were some ideas you got for creating a display?

Problem Log Questions

Which display that you observed fit the theme of the exhibit the best? How do you think the display was able to do that?

Lesson 14

Exhibit Display Construction

LESSON LENGTH: 1 session planning; several sessions research and construction

INSTRUCTIONAL PURPOSE

- To extend student skills in independent study.
- To facilitate synthesis of information into museum displays.

MATERIALS AND HANDOUTS

Independent Study Project Folders
Videocamera

Handout 14.1: "Need to Know" board
Handout 14.2: Problem Log Questions
      Handout 14.3: Problem Log Questions
      Handout 14.4: Problem Log Questions
      Handout 14.5: Problem Log Questions

Session 1

THINGS TO DO

1. With the new information about the museum and artifacts from the simulated dig in hand, students should be ready to start tackling the museum display. Ask students to list the various parts of the museum display and help them map the large, overall structure of the display.

2. Help students divide the things to do into discrete tasks. Either assign the tasks to individuals or groups or let students choose areas of interest to be their job in construction of the display.

THINGS TO ASK

- Now that we have this new information, how are we going to design the museum display?

- What are the topics of the display supposed to be?

- What are some ways that we can combine talking about the dig and about the two cultures?

- How big should the display be? Where should we set it up?

- What are the different pieces of work that will have to be completed in order to finish the display?

- Should everyone work on all parts of the display or should we divide the jobs among us?

Subsequent Sessions

THINGS TO DO

1. Meet with individual students and/or groups to decide specific tasks and complete an Independent Study Project Folder. Include both tasks to complete and a time line. Independent Study Project Folders should be kept during the independent study to monitor progress. Folders can be used as the basis for student-teacher conferences.

2. Work with the independent groups as they conduct research and prepare different parts of the museum display (display of artifacts, preparation of display descriptions, art work to go with the display, outline for docent presentation).

3. From time to time, meet with the class in a large group to do a progress report. Allow students to air frustrations in the large group to encourage interaction and cooperation between groups as well as within groups. Also have the large group generate a list of people they would like to invite to see the display.

4. All students should be required to be a docent and to walk someone through the display. This activity will act as a culminating assessment for this sub-problem and will also help students develop oral communication skills. Plenty of practice time should be allowed for this activity, with students listening to one another and providing feedback for improvement.

5. Class Museum of Archaeological Studies can be open for tours during an evening parents' meeting. At this time, students can present their work as if they are museum docents in a national museum. Each student can be videotaped during the evening.

6. A subsequent class evaluation de-briefing session can be held to watch the videotape of the student presentations and do a peer evaluation based on criteria for research, product, and presentation.

ASSESSMENT

1. Problem logs.
2. Independent study folders.
3. Actual museum presentation.

What do we know?	What do we need to know?	How can we find out?

PROBLEM LOG QUESTIONS

Putting together a museum display is pretty complicated! What thing is easiest for you right now? Which is most frustrating? What ideas do you have to make things better?

How well do you think you did on your practice presentation of the exhibit? What areas will you concentrate on when you practice?

HANDOUT 14.4

PROBLEM LOG QUESTIONS

How well is the group working? What are the tasks which you are working on right now? What are the best ways to work together?

HANDOUT 14.5

PROBLEM LOG QUESTIONS

What have you learned about how museums displays are made? Is it easy work? Hard?
What are the easiest and hardest things about making a display?

School Sub-Problem

LESSON LENGTH: 1 session

INSTRUCTIONAL PURPOSE

- To introduce the school sub-problem.

MATERIALS AND HANDOUTS

Resource books and people
Print and human resources for information gathering

Handout 15.1: "Need to Know" board
Handout 15.2: Letter from the School Superintendent
> Handout 15.3: Problem Log Questions
> Handout 15.4: Problem Log Questions
> Handout 15.5: Problem Log Questions

Session 1

THINGS TO DO

1. Give students a copy of the Letter from the School Superintendent. Use the "Need to Know" board to clarify the new information and new questions which emerge from the sub-problem.

2. Derive with the entire class the set of questions that people on either side of the issue would have to answer in order to justify their position.

3. Introduce to students the variety of different kinds of criteria that could be used to determine whether a decision is "good." Provide examples of how the ways to make decisions (attached) could be used to help figure out whether or not a solution works.

ASSESSMENT

Problem Log describing new areas of the problem.

Session 2

THINGS TO DO

1. Inform students that they will now look at the problem from different perspectives in order to start shaping a resolution (from the builder, construction worker, student at the new school, etc.).

2. Discuss with students what they "Need to Know" in order to decide whether or not to continue the dig. The instructor should be sure that students also begin to think about what will constitute a "good" solution (How will you know which solution is best? Do you think there might be a compromise position possible? What do you think that might be?).

3. Introduce the idea of bias and how bias could affect how different people think about the issue.

THINGS TO ASK

- What new problem(s) are presented to us in this new situation?

- What do we need to know to understand what is going on?

- Is the superintendent right to try to stop the dig?

- What is his point of view?

- Is that the only point of view that needs to be considered?

- What are other possible points of view?

- Could we find people who look at things the same way as this superintendent?

- Who would they be?

- How could we go about finding out what people in these categories might think about the issue?

- Who could act as a resource person for us on this part of the problem?
- Who would represent the point of view of the archaeologist?
- What questions will you ask them?
- How will you describe the situation to them?
- What is a "good" decision?
- What are the things you will want to consider as you work?
- What are the most important issues for the group you represent?
- What would an "ideal" solution for your group look like?
- Which of the decision areas is most suited to your group's position?
- What other decision areas should they be considering?

ASSESSMENT

Problem Log entry defining the problem.

HANDOUT 15.1

"NEED TO KNOW" BOARD

What do we know?	What do we need to know?	How can we find out?

James City County School System

555 Education Place
Williamsburg, Virginia 23188
Telephone: 804/555-3233   FAX 804/555-8892

Dr. William J. Workman, Superintendent

Archaeological Museum
College of William and Mary
Willliamsburg, Virginia 23815

To Whom It May Concern:

I write this letter out of concern for the delay in the construction of the new elementary school in our district. As members of the community, I'm sure you know that the school is very badly needed. Without the new facility, class size in this district will increase from 25 children to 30 children per classroom. In addition, four classes which are now in trailers will have to stay in trailers instead of being in a real school. I am very much afraid that this will hurt the education of children who live in our area.

Another concern is for the teachers who expect to work in the new building. If the school cannot open on schedule, I will have to tell them that I cannot hire them this fall. A total of 20 teachers, plus the school principal, vice principal, 2 secretaries and the school nurse will not have jobs if the school does not start on time. In order for the school to be finished on time, construction must start again by the beginning of next week.

I'm sure that the information you are finding in your dig is interesting, but it can't be as important as a new school! Your information is only about the past, the community needs to think about the future. Please stop work on the dig now.

Sincerely,

William J. Workman, Ph.D.
Superintendent

Evaluate our problem statement based on this new information. Would you like to change it or keep it the same? Why? What changes would you make? Why?

HANDOUT 15.4

PROBLEM LOG QUESTIONS

Add the new information and new connections to your original problem web. Describe the changes you have made.

PROBLEM LOG QUESTIONS

Looks like things have changed again! The Museum Director would like to know what the problem is now! Describe for the Museum Director how the problem has changed since the dig was found. Is it still the same problem?

Problem Resolution: Town Meeting

LESSON LENGTH: 1 session presentation; 1 session de-brief

INSTRUCTIONAL PURPOSE

- To resolve the problem

MATERIALS AND HANDOUTS

Student prepared visual aids

Handout 16.1: Problem Log Questions
Handout 16.2: Problem Log Questions
Handout 16.3: Town Meeting Planning Form

Session 1

THINGS TO DO

1. Have students prepare presentations to try to convince the town council that a permanent dig site should be created or the dig should be halted and the school should be built.

2. Student presentations should be made in the context of a town meeting. Ideally, students should make their presentation to real members of the community (a teacher, a principal, a parent, a professor, a museum representative) who could give students some authentic feedback on their arguments. Alternatively, some students can be provided with roles ahead of time that would fit the various constituencies represented in the argument.

3. At the conclusion of the presentations, students should be asked to come to consensus about what could happen. Introduce the possibility of a compromise position. Can students reach a viable compromise? What would either side be able to "give" in order to reach a compromise?

THINGS TO ASK

- What are the main points being made by the pro-school side? By the pro-dig side?

- Are all of their concerns different? Is there room to try to find a situation that would be acceptable to both groups?

- How will you know if you've reached an acceptable compromise?

- How are you going to go about trying to reach a compromise?

Session 2

THINGS TO DO

1. Discuss the compromise position with students. Is it what they expected it to be? If they did not reach a compromise, ask what arguments could not be resolved and if there were goals of the two groups that were mutually exclusive.

2. Have students look at their final resolution relative to the five ethical appeals. Ask students which of the appeal(s) is most clearly represented in the resolution, and which least. Discuss the reason why the different appeals were or were not important to the resolution.

3. Ask students about the process of reaching a compromise. Which parts were most difficult? Which easiest? Lead students to state which strategies facilitated the compromise process and which impeded the process. Ask students to make some generalizations about negotiation and group work based on their experience.

THINGS TO ASK

- How do you feel about your compromise position?
- Did either side get everything they wanted?
- What short- and long-term consequences will your decision have?
- What did you learn about the process of compromising?
- What made things go smoothly?
- What made the process more difficult?

ASSESSMENT

1. Town meeting presentations.
2. De-briefing discussions.
3. Problem log activities.

PROBLEM LOG QUESTIONS

In your opinion, was either side absolutely right or absolutely wrong? Why? Why not? What were the positive arguments on either side?

Think about the way the group worked to get a compromise position. What was the most successful thing the group did? What was the thing that got in the way the most?

TOWN MEETING PLANNING FORM

Why should the town council vote for your side of the issue?

What data do you have to support your side of the issue?

What will happen if your side of the issue loses?

What display can help convince the town council to vote for your side of the issue?

Final Overall Unit Assessment Activity

INSTRUCTIONAL PURPOSE

- To assess understanding of archaeology.
- To assess the ability of the student to use appropriate scientific process skills in the resolution of a real-world problem.
- To assess student understanding of the concept of systems.

ESTIMATED TIME

The content assessment should take the students approximately thirty minutes; the experimental design assessment should take the students approximately thirty minutes; and the systems assessment should take the students approximately thirty minutes.

MATERIALS AND HANDOUTS

Handout 17.1: Final Content Assessment

Handout 17.2: Experimental Design Assessment

Handout 17.3: Systems Assessment

Scoring protocols for Final Content Assessment, Experimental Design Assessment, and Systems Assessment

PROCEDURE

Have students complete assessments found in Handouts 17.1, 17.2, and 17.3.

HANDOUT 17.1

FINAL CONTENT ASSESSMENT (30 MINUTES)

1. What is an artifact? Give a definition and an example.

2. Why is a notebook one of an archaeologist's most important tools?

3. Name another piece of equipment that would be useful to an archaeologist and describe how it is used.

4A. Why is artifact theft a problem for archaeologists?

4B. Why do Native Americans see artifact theft as a problem?

5A. Suppose you found what you thought could be an archaeological site. Who would you tell, and why?

5B. Why would it be important for you not to disturb anything at the site?

HANDOUT 17.2

EXPERIMENTAL DESIGN ASSESSMENT (30 MINUTES)

You and your best friend are building a treehouse, and have borrowed some of your dad's nails. As you are hammering two boards together, your friend asks you whether the nails are galvanized or not. You say "What's galvanized?" and he tells you that galvanized nails won't rust, while regular nails will rust and eventually fall apart if they get wet. Since you live in Seattle where it rains a lot, you can see that this is an important question. You don't want to ask your dad because he doesn't know that you borrowed his nails yet. What experiment could you do to see whether the nails are galvanized?

1. What experiment could you do that would allow you to test this idea? In your answer, include the following:

   a. Your hypothesis:

   b. The materials you would need:

   c. The protocol you would use:

   d. A data table showing what data you would collect:

   e. A description of how you would use your data to decide whether your idea was correct.

HANDOUT 17.3

SYSTEMS ASSESSMENT (30 MINUTES)

You can think of the treehouse as a system.

1. List the parts of the system in the spaces provided below. Include boundaries, elements, input, and output.
   Boundaries:

   Elements:

   Input:

   Output:

2. Draw a diagram of the system that shows where each of the parts can be found.

3. On your diagram, draw lines (in a different color) showing three important interactions between different parts of the treehouse system. Why is each of these interactions important to the system? Explain your answer.
   a. Interaction #1:

   b. Interaction #2:

   c. Interaction #3:

189

SCORING PROTOCOL
FINAL CONTENT ASSESSMENT

1. **(10 points)** What is an artifact? Give a definition and an example.

   An artifact is any object that was made or modified by humans; examples could include flint arrowheads, pottery, personal computers.

   Scoring: Give 5 points for the definition and 5 points for any reasonable example.

2. **(10 points)** Archaeologists use many different kinds of equipment.

   a. **(5 points)** Why is a notebook one of an archaeologist's most important tools?

   Recording all data relevant to each artifact discovered is as important as finding the artifacts themselves: they are useless unless their position in the archaeological system is known.

   Scoring: Accept any answer that makes it clear that information about the artifact's position, appearance, and so on is important to the interpretation of an artifact's meaning for the system.

   b. Name another piece of equipment that would be useful to an archaeologist and describe how it is used.

   Brushes, scrapers, sieves, cameras, etc.
   Scoring: Accept all reasonable answers.

3. **(10 points)** Archaeologists study many different human cultures. What is the difference between prehistoric and historic cultures, and how is study of historic cultures easier?

   Prehistoric cultures left no documents, while historic cultures leave a written record. The existence of a written record makes these cultures easier to understand.

4. **(10 points)** In the Southwestern United States, Native American artifacts are frequently stolen from archaeological sites by people who collect these artifacts as art. This illegal activity is a problem both for archaeologists and for living Native Americans.

   a. **(5 points)** Why is artifact theft a problem for archaeologists?

   When the artifacts are stolen, any information about their place in the archaeological system is lost; thus the archaeologists lose potential understanding of the culture that left the artifacts. Artifact hunters frequently destroy what they don't take, so the archaeological sites are rendered useless.

Scoring: Accept any answer that makes it clear that the student understands the importance of the context of the site to the interpretation of an artifact's meaning.

b. **(5 points)** Why do Native Americans see artifact theft as a problem?

Many of the artifacts and archaeological sites have symbolic or sacred value to the Native Americans whose ancestors created them; artifact hunters thus destroy the heritage of living Native Americans.

5. **(10 points)** Suppose you found what you thought could be an archaeological site.

a. **(5 points)** Who would you tell, and why?

A responsible adult: a parent, a teacher, an archaeology professor . . . if the site is going to be treated properly, eventually an archaeologist needs to know about it, and if the student can't tell an archaeologist about it, they need to tell an adult who can.

Scoring: Accept any reasonable answer.

b. **(5 points)** Why would it be important for you not to disturb anything at the site?

Disturbing the site means losing archaeological information. Because I am a young student, I don't have the training needed to treat the site properly, and I need to leave it alone.

Scoring: Accept any answer that makes it clear that the student knows that information could be lost if the site was disturbed by an untrained person.

Total number of points possible: 50

SCORING PROTOCOL
EXPERIMENTAL DESIGN

You and your best friend are building a treehouse, and have borrowed some of your dad's nails. As you are hammering two boards together, your friend asks you whether the nails are galvanized or not. You say "What's galvanized?" and he tells you that galvanized nails won't rust, while regular nails will rust and eventually fall apart if they get wet. Since you live in Seattle where it rains a lot, you can see that this is an important question. You don't want to ask your dad because he doesn't know that you borrowed his nails yet. What experiment could you do to see whether the nails are galvanized?

In your answer, include the following:

a. **(5 points)** Your hypothesis:

The nails are not galvanized.

(**Note:** Other hypotheses are possible; accept all reasonable answers; give five points for any reasonable hypothesis.)

b. **(10 points)** The materials you would need, including any necessary safety equipment:

Some of the nails that you "borrowed"
Money
Ungalvanized nails (from the hardware store)
Galvanized nails (from the hardware store)
Containers
Water

(**Note:** The student only needs to list the above materials; this materials list does not need to be comprehensive. Accept all reasonable materials lists, as long as they're consonant with the hypothesis in part a.)

c. **(10 points)** The protocol you would use:

I would buy a few galvanized nails and a few ungalvanized nails at the hardware store, and keep them in labeled containers so that I remembered which was which. I would then set up three labeled containers as follows: the first would contain some (5–10) of the galvanized nails in water, the second would contain the same number of ungalvanized nails in water, and the third would contain the same number of "borrowed" nails in water. I would check the nails in the containers each day for signs of rust and record my results. When the ungalvanized nails had been rusty for two weeks, I would end my experiment.

Scoring: Give five points for any reasonable protocol (or experimental outline: not every step need be listed in fine detail, but it should be clear what the student intends to test) that is consonant with the hypothesis given in part a (if the two seem to be unrelated, withold these points); give five points for the presence of a control for the experiment.

Note: This experiment has two controls: the positive control, namely the ungalvanized nails, which should rust, and the negative control, namely the galvanized nails, which should not rust.

d. **(15 points)** A data table showing what data you would collect:

#Rusty nails in the containers:

Date	Galvanized	Ungalvanized	"Borrowed"

Scoring: Give five points for the presence of a data table; 5 points if there is an independent variable (not necessarily labeled as such) present in the data table headings; and 5 points if there is at least one dependent variable (not necessarily labeled as such) present in the data table headings. In this answer, the type of nail used is the independent variable, and the number of rusty nails is the dependent variable.

(**Note:** Accept all reasonable answers, as long as they're consonant with the student's answers to parts a–d)

e. **(10 points)** A description of how you would use your data to decide whether the nails that you borrowed were galvanized or not.

I would let the experiment run until the ungalvanized control nails had all been rusty for two weeks. If, as expected, my galvanized control nails had not rusted, I would assume that the experiment was working well. If my "borrowed" nails had rusted by the end of the experiment, I would conclude that they were ungalvanized and buy some galvanized nails to reinforce the treehouse. If they hadn't rusted, I would conclude that they were galvanized.

Scoring: Give ten points for an answer that explains how the data will be used to come up with a conclusion. If the student doesn't mention the data, then give no points.

(**Note:** Accept all reasonable answers, as long as they're consonant with the student's answers to parts a–d.)

Total number of points possible: 50

Scoring Protocol

Systems Assessment

A house is a system.

1. **(25 points total)** List the parts of the system. Include boundaries, elements, input, and output.

   Boundaries (describe): The outside edges of the house (the surfaces of outside walls, doors, and so on).

   Scoring: For ten points, accept any reasonable *closed* boundaries.

   Elements (list at least five): siding, brick, walls, doors, windows heating system, cooling system, termites in the porch floor.

   Scoring: Give one point for each reasonable element consistent with the boundaries up to a maximum of five points.

   Input (list at least two kinds): air from outside, heat from the sun, rain dripping on the roof, moss growing on the brickwork.

   Scoring: Give 2.5 points for each listed input item consistent with the boundaries up to a maximum of five points.

   Output (list at least two kinds): heat from the inside through the air conditioning system; combustion fumes from the furnace; indoor air released from windows and doors.

   Scoring: Give 2.5 points for each listed output item consistent with the boundaries, up to five points.

2. **(10 points)** Draw a diagram of the system that shows where each of the parts can be found.

   Scoring: Accept any reasonable diagram that includes the system components listed in the answer to question 1.

3. **(15 points total)** On your diagram, draw lines (in a different color) showing three important interactions between different parts of the system. Why is each of these interactions important to the system? Explain your answer.

   a. Interaction #1: The indoor air interacts with thermostat components; if it is cold, it cools the thermostat, and in the winter, this results in the furnace turning on; in the summer, warm air interacting with the thermostat causes the air conditioning to go on.

b. Interaction #2: Solar heat interacts with house components to warm the house.

c. Interaction#3: Termites eventually eat the porch floor and cause it to collapse.

(Accept any reasonable interaction; give five points for each correct answer.)

Total number of points possible: 50

Suggested Unit Extensions

Students can research the work of a well known archaeologist. Suggestions might include:

Sir Francis Petrie

Heinrich Schleimann

Sir Arthur Evans

Howard Carter

John Lloyd Stephens

Students can investigate significant dig sites and the reason for their significance. Suggestions might include:

Pompeii—Italy

Knossos—Crete

Thebes—Egypt

Peat Bogs—Denmark

Stonehenge—England

Mesopotamia

Hanging Gardens of Babylon

Altamira—Spain

Athens—Greece

Tune—Norway

Hsien-yang—China

Mediterranean Sea—Turkey

Zimbabwe—Rhodesia

Nazca Plain—Peru

Mohenjo-daro—India

Lascaux—France

Part III

REFERENCES

UNIT REFERENCES

Association for Great Lakes Maritime History. *Finders keepers: Preserving Great Lakes shipwrecks.* South Haven, MI.

Barrows, H. (1988). *The tutorial process.* Springfield, IL: Southern Illinois University Press.

Barry, I. (1981). *Discovering archaeology.* London: Stonehenge Press, Inc.

Bray, W. & Trump, D. (1970). *The American heritage guide to archaeology.* NY: American Heritage Press.

Calver, W.L. & Bolton, R.P. (1950). *History written with pick and shovel.* NY: New York Historical Society.

Colonial Williamsburg Foundation (Producer) (1978). *The Williamsburg file.* (Video) Available from Kartes Video Communications, Indianapolis, IN.

Colonial Williamsburg Foundation (Producer) (1969). *Archaeologists at work.* (Video) Available from Kartes Video Communications, Indianapolis, IN.

Colonial Williamsburg Foundation (Producer) (1969). *Doorway to the past* (Video) Available from Kartes Video Communications, Indianapolis, IN.

Cooke, J. (1987). *Archaeology.* NY: The Bookwright Press.

Cothron, J.H., Giese, R.N., & Rezba, R.J. (1989). *Students and research: Practical suggestions for science classrooms and competitions.* Dubuque, IA: Kendall/Hunt, Inc.

Cotter, J.L. (1958). *Archaeological excavations at Jamestown, Virginia.* Washington, DC: U.S. Government Printing Office.

Cottrell, L. (1964). *Digs and diggers.* Cleveland, OH: The World Publishing Company.

Deetz, J. (1967). *Invitation to archaeology.* Garden City, NY: The American Museum of Natural History.

Dekock, P. (Ed.) (1982). Small things forgotten: A simulation of the archeological reconstruction of a vanished civilization. *DBA Interact.* Lakeside, CA: Interaction Publications, Inc.

Federal Law Enforcement Training Center. *Assault on time.*

Fraden, D.B. (1983). *Archaeology.* Chicago, IL: Children's Press.

Gibson, M. (1980). *A new look at mysteries of archaeology.* NY: Arco Publishing, Inc.

Gorenstein, S. (1965). *Introduction to archaeology.* NY: Basic Books, Inc.

Griffin, J.B. (Ed.) (1952). *Archaeology of Eastern United States.* Chicago, IL: The University of Chicago Press.

Hackwell, J.W. (1986). *Digging to the past.* NY: Charles Scribner's & Sons.

Hackwell, J.W. (1988). *Diving to the past.* NY: Charles Scribner's & Sons.

Harrington, J.C. (1965). *Archaeology and the historical society.* Nashville, TN: The American Association for State and Local History.

Heizer, R.F. & Graham, J.A. (1967). *A guide to field methods in archaeology.* Palo Alto, CA: The National Press.

Hudson, J.P. & Cotter, J.L. (1957). *New discoveries at Jamestown.* Washington, DC: U.S. Government Printing Office.

Hume, N.I. (1962). *Excavations at Rosewell*. Washington, DC: Smithsonian Institution.

Hume, N.I. (1965). *Excavations at Clay Bank*. Washington, DC: Smithsonian Institution.

Hume, N.I. (1968). *Here lies Virginia*. NY: Alfred A. Knopf.

Hume, N.I. (1969). *Historical archaeology: Guide to artifacts*. NY: Alfred A. Knopf.

Morrison, V.F. (1981). *Going on a dig*. NY: Dodd, Mead & Company.

Pearson, M. Licorice stick half-life dating. *Science experiments facts on file*. NY: Facts on File, Inc.

Pickering, R. (1989). *I can be an archaeologist*. Chicago, IL: Children's Press.

Plenderleith, H.J. (1956). *The conservation of antiquities and works of art: Treatment, repair, and restoration*. London: Oxford University Press.

Porell, B. (1979). *Digging the past*. Reading, MA: Addison-Wesley.

Rainey, D. (1990). *American history? It's beneath your feet!*

Robbins, M. & Irving, M.B. (1973). *The amateur archaeologist's handbook*. New York: Thomas Y. Crowell Company.

Rollin, S. (1982). *The illustrated atlas, archaeology*. NY: Warwick Press.

Silverwood Films. *Ground trust: Archaeology in the city*. Philadelphia, PA.

Stark, R. (1986). *Archaeology*. Hawthorne, NJ: Educational Impressions, Inc.

Stuart, G. (1979). *Secrets from the past*. National Geographic Society.

United States Department of the Interior, National Park Service (1991). *Archaeology and education: The classroom and beyond*. Washington, DC: Author.

Watkins, C.M. (1968). *The cultural history of Marlborough*. Washington, DC: Smithsonian Institution Press.

Watkins, C.M. (1969). *North Devon pottery and its export to America in the 17th century*. Washington, DC: Smithsonian Institution.

Watkins, C.M. & Hume, N.I. (1967). *The poor potter of Yorktown*. Washington, DC: Smithsonian Institution.

Ymah, M. (1993). *Dig this! How archaeologists unearth our past*. Minneapolis, MN: Rhinestone Press.

Other Bibliographic Sources

Listing of education in archaeological programs: The LEAP Clearinghouse by Patricia Knoll, Archaeological Assistance Division, National Park Service, 1991. Publication Number PB91180067. Paper—$36.50 plus a handling fee; microfiche—$12.50 plus a handling fee (also 1992—Publication Number PB 93213460. Paper—$27.00 plus a handling fee; microfiche—$12.50 plus a handling fee.)

Classroom sources for archaeology education, a resource guide. Education Resource Forum, contact K.C. Smith, Museum of Florida History, 500 S. Bronough Street, Tallahassee, FL 32399-0250; (904) 487-3711.